Sandhurst Occasional Papers

No 14

Looking-Glass Leadership

Dr Patrick Mileham

Central Library
Royal Military Academy Sandhurst
2013

'Something's going to happen'

'Good Leadership always exists in a form appropriate to its environment'. John Adair[1]

Forgive the double entendre in the title. Agreed, it's a means of grasping your imagination, but it also has a firm place in the bibliography of world literature. The 'looking-glass' story is a neat metaphor about today's complex even chaotic circumstances, events and relationships amongst which all leaders, including military leaders, lead – a subject about which it is virtually impossible to write anything definite or definitive. Abstract nouns frequently have a multiplicity of meanings, more comfortable in a thesaurus than a dictionary. Does the very word definition imply that there ought to be a narrowing down to only one true meaning? The art of leading is almost as wide as human nature, even if a leader in his or her way is unique.

Despite recognizing intuitively that environments shift, over the past dozen years the British Army has tried to write normative theory, something like doctrine, on what is an abstract noun, leadership. The exercise has so far failed[2]. Management gurus have devise scores, hundreds, maybe thousands of theories, principles, models, frameworks and templates, trying to find something like the exact truth about leading. Like traditional military plans, so many of them do not long survive the first lethal encounter with the enemy, particularly in the reality of the work of the armed forces.

What's in the title? The obvious answer is that thinking leaders, which should include all professional people, need the discipline of introspection. In short they need the advice of Robert Burns, to hold up a mirror and look honestly at themselves as others see them. They need minds which watch

---

[1] John Adair, Training for leadership, Macdonald, London, 1968, pp 21-22 and 139.
[2] As a descriptive, not a normative publication, *Developing Leaders. A Sandhurst Guide*, 2012, is highly commended. In British doctrine. leadership is deemed to be a dynamic in the 'moral component' of military capability, inter-related with the' physical' and 'intellectual' components .

themselves, to paraphrase Albert Camus, observing themselves as if in a play, a dramatic performance, acting their part. Mastering themselves, they qualify to develop others.

But context is all, as John Adair asserts, and modern life is no more certain than it has ever been. We find that much of the time we seem to live in a world *behind* the looking-glass, where so much is unreal that truth becomes almost impossible to grasp. Day by day, to quote Lewis Carroll, life becomes 'curiouser and curiouser'. The unfolding chronology of cause and effect - particularly about our security – sometimes hardly accords with common sense, and paralysis occurs. We seem to have little or no real control over the unfolding drama. We find the stark competitive duality and often dark side of human nature. We witness the forces of evil, and actions of other people whose minds we cannot understand, or understand them too well but cannot do anything about them and their activities. We find it mystifying that those against us also think they are working towards an ideal world, different to ours and so often the complete opposite of our ideal world.

In Carroll's tales, the heroine finds an underlying pattern firstly in a pack of cards. However nothing is as it ought to be. Wonderland is perhaps an analogy for national politics, arbitrary power, social custom and laws – including physical laws - that, *prima facie,* are sensible, but actually incomprehensible. The second tale is based on the battle-space of a chess board. Any rules of engagement are tested to near destruction. In the absurd, knock-about fighting the players seem to accept without question the reason for fighting, *Jus ad bellum,* 'exactly like a riddle with no ending'. The nature of fighting, *Jus in bello,* is depicted in the 'state of mind that wants to deny something, only doesn't know what to deny'.

To be serious, while these are direct quotations from Carroll, they are pertinent comments applicable to us in the often acute insecurities we face today. People encountered in the stories play parts that are surreal. They behave with chaotic incoherency but according to their own mentalities working with supreme confidence even gravitas. They have some sort of intent towards an ending which they believe is right, but word for word to the reader presents a state of dreamlike inconsequence. 'Everything's got a moral if only you can find it' passes for doctrine and belief-system. 'Take care of yourself! Something's going to happen!' Happily Carroll does not give us a true horror story. There is no bloodshed. There are no real terrorists, suicide bombers, IEDs or drones in his novels. We know Alice will come back home to a world where reality is closer to something we identify as the truth.

Chaos and Complexity

'We ought to continue to keep in mind our great object the genuine peace and tranquillity of the world, in our view and shape our arrangements so as to provide for it'[3]. Arthur, Duke of Wellington.

Delving for explanations of our modern world, we have to accept and understand something called chaos theory. Once we have conquered our fear of chaos we discover another bundle of already complicated dynamics working exponentially, which we call the theory of complexity[4]. We now have to think not only deductively and inductively at the same time, but also more than ever in the use of 'pragmatism...a practical way of doing philosophy'[5]. This falls into what Isaiah Berlin describes as basket three[6], needed to grasp and understand anything and everything about the vast personal, social, physiological, political, economic and global-ecological demands of our Darwinian world.

---

[3] Letter to a friend, quoted in Sir Nevile Henderson, *Failure of a Mission'* Hodder and Stoughton, London 1940, p.94.
[4] The intellectual study of 'Chaos' and 'Complexity' is gaining ground; hitherto such details were thought of as random phenomena.
[5] Professor Huw Price, *Cambridge Journal*, No 68, March 2013, p25.
[6] Isaiah Berlin, *The Power of Ideas*, London, Random House, 200

Our view of the world is of course influenced by all the philosophers from history and of today, working on existential and ontological questions, drawn from the beliefs of religious leaders, such as the Old Testament fathers, Christ, Mohammed, the Buddha and Confucius, who each argued for the best of moral conduct amongst their adherents, linked more or less to universal principles. At worst traditionalized thoughts are further modified, ranging from apocalyptic threats and evil intent, to deconstructive and nihilistic insults by radical religious zealots. Humanists, atheists and pagans of today add to the confusion of ideas. The middle way, found in Berlin's basket three, is about wisdom and moderation, based on practical means derived from the classic virtues, to balance our looking-glass and real worlds.

Life moves at a fast pace. Observing closely we are told that the finely detailed phenomena of chaos and complexity are caused by emerging factors in daily family, social, community, national and international life. They are becoming more and more dynamic and interactive, interdependent yet contradictory, ambiguous, paradoxical and diverse. But we also have to compound all the above factors with a deepening study of psychology, philosophy, international law and the spirit of constitutional governance, together with the dynamics of individual human rights in the context of competitive market forces.

Advanced democracy we know has a basis in optimistic but also counterfactual idealism. We no longer live in a world which once seemed straightforward, with the causes and effects of human intentions and actions as simple and linear. For some time we have understood that there are now far more known unknowns and unknown unknowns than we ever imagined. They are incremental.

To this mix we also have to add the possibility of being able successfully to resolve violence by force, and find some sort of sense in the confusion of today's and tomorrow's world. With inequalities and distorting diversities we believe the world is not yet ready for pacifism. Indeed much of the world is not yet ready to accept universal human rights or even the notion of fundamental freedom for all.

Sure, we know war is evil, looking-glass or no looking-glass. The paradox of all paradoxes is to use force to stop the use of force. How do military professional persons act against evil-doers? A cry such as to 'take life to save a life'[7], we are told roughly speaking, is a simplified justification for the use of lethal and proportional force. Our soldiers encounter many 'wicked problems', not covered by the rules of engagement. They have to conduct themselves balancing 'fighting spirit' with 'courageous restraint' - both categorically Clausewitzian 'moral forces' - to cope with the conundrums met on the battlefields of Iraq and Afghanistan, in accord with moral principles of 'proportional force' and 'double effect'. 'Do as you ought, not as you want'[8] (deontological advice); 'think to the finish' (teleological guidance); exponential, computer assessments and algorithms of cause and effect (assisting in resolving the ambiguities of consequentialism) all these shorthand expressions, methods and analogues emphasize that military operations are indeed frustratingly algebraic[9]. There is no neat equation of our 'effects based capability' versus the enemy's 'effects based capability'. It is complicated by the extra, and truly humane factor of altruism, supposedly on our side, of generating 'force for good' [10] which we believe is necessary to win and bring conflicts to a happy ending. Which side is the less naïve, us or them?

---

[7] Prince Harry of Wales, interviewed for BBC news, 21 January 2013.

[8] Quoted by Major-General Patrick Marriott, (Commandant The Royal Military Academy, Sandhurst) Defence Academy /Royal College of Defence Studies Ethics Seminar, 4 November 2012.

[9] Tolstoy deduced that the art of command was a process algebraic in nature. His experience was of the Crimean war, which one could argue was fought with traditional linear thinking, whereas the American Civil War, a handful of years later was the first war in modern times fought on non-linear principles. See W.B Gallie, *Philosophers of Peace and War*, Cambridge University Press, 1979, p. 111.

[10] The declared 'United Kingdom Defence Vision', extant in 2013, but always of embarrassment to serving members of the British Armed Forces.

Contemporary military operations

'The "conflict paradigm" has shifted and we must adapt our approaches if we are to succeed'. Ministry of Defence[11].

Enough of metaphor and meta-theory; what about reality and truth? What are today's military encounters and who are the enemies? We seem to throw armed forces into military operations to simplify and deal conclusively with a problem. We are often disappointed with the results. We engage in 'information operations' and 'cyber warfare' because we have to. Asymmetric capability of force does not make our enemy our friend. We use unmanned aerial vehicles, 'drones', to save lives on one hand and take lives on the other. Moral maybe, but ethically dubious[12].

What about the 'moral' and 'conceptual components' of our military capability and effectiveness? Even if the enemies' 'physical component'[13] of violent capability and effect is obvious, where do their 'conceptual' and 'moral' components lie? They deliver death and destruction with devilish cunning, with horror tactics. Formalized a hundred years ago when the world seemed to run on the principles of railway timetables, surprise became a traditional military principle of war, which we used to think belonged exclusively to us. Now the element of perpetual surprise belongs to the terrorist, whether a substantial group with critical mass and a politico-military agenda, or individuals acting alone or virtually alone.

For instance our armed forces were sent to the Balkans from 1992, with a deliberately soft power mandate, which worked in Cyprus 20 years earlier,

---

[11] MOD, Defence Concepts and Doctrine Centre (DCDC), Strategic Trends Programme. *Future Character of Conflict,* 2010, p.1.

[12] Moral and ethical motivations and results are not coterminous. The former derives from Latin *mos,* (pl) *mores,* leading to the community's distinction of right and wrong, and the latter derived from the Greek *ethos, ethikos,* a process of mind reaching for universal distinction between good and bad.

[13] MOD, DCDC, *British Defence Doctrine,* Edn. 4, 2011. These three components are derived from Clausewitz.

but exposed British and allied soldiers to extra danger, physical, legal and moral. Which side were the good guys, they asked? It was only resolved when lethal force could be used, particularly during the last months of the 1999 liberation of Kosovo, with decisive aerial bombardment by NATO and, surprisingly, a virtually bloodless ground manoeuvre. A stable peace was achieved, if not for all parties a happy one.

Fortunately the right level of physical force quickly ended the Sierra Leone (2001) conflict. Not so in Iraq in 2003, where the method of intervention-invasion was swift in the event. However the world could not work out whether it was liberation, which the Americans initially thought, or an uncomfortable continuous belligerent occupation. For the British contingent this uncertainty led to disarray in Basra, when the Iranian-backed Mahdi militia seized the conceptual-physical-moral high ground, causing an inelegant, perhaps humiliating, British withdrawal.

Two years later the Secretary of State sent in the British armed forces in great numbers into Afghanistan to bring stability without expecting any sort of fire-fight. Surprise? That happened in due course in Helmand Province, which required the most intense fire power to be used by British troops since 1945, some commanders alleged. Now the semi-passive, proxy-patrolling method, benign but hardly an easy one, is used to bring stabilization. Named the 'mentoring' role, on occasions the mentored have turn against and killed their mentoring agents. A lethal oxymoron? Command has now (June 2013) passed to the Afghans. 'War amongst the people', or more technically, 'culture-centric warfare'[14], is the setting and forms an interpretation of what has happened in the Balkans, Iraq and Afghanistan in recent years. After Afghanistan we have to wonder, what next?

---

[14] These expressions respectively were raised by UK General Sir Rupert Smith in *The Utility of Force: The Art of War in the Modern World*,, Random House, London, 2005 and US General Robert Statement to Congress Scales, 2004, see www.au.af.mil/au/awc/awcgate/congress/04-07-15scales.pdf accessed 24 March 2013.

Ambiguous, contradictory, paradoxical, oxymoronic, we have to accept that the world has changed much since our youth. To seize each day we can sense dynamics that are becoming incrementally novel and unpredictable. In truth our world is in chaos. No one appears to be really in charge of anything. Counter-intuitively, surprisingly, when people keep their nerve the world, somehow, seems to work. I started by writing about thinking leaders. Are there to few or too many? Perhaps there is something to be gained from understanding endless opposites, which Heraclitus optimistically said 'could be united by change'. This requires informed observers and leaders not only to look *in* the mirror, but *through* the looking-glass of one's own mind and that of national *Realpolitik*.

Questions for leaders.

'Derived from the early Italian risicare, *which means to dare... risk is a choice rather than a fate'[15]*. Peter Bernstein.

The answer of course is that leaders exist and they are needed to handle both people and risk. How do leaders lead amid all this complexity, in fact as well as in theory? A leader is someone who simplifies factors whenever possible in his or her own mind, but also those of their teams and subordinates, without being simplistic. He or she then has the task of encouraging others to take action in real time and real place amongst real people. Does technology, particularly digital technology help? Virtual leadership? What about the 'mentoring' process in operations already referred to? Leading by proxy perhaps, or leadership-transfer? Much of what the forces of evil do, amongst which our armed forces operate, are beyond sight and normal human understanding, and even state-of-the-art technology. Some events are almost unimaginable, until they happen. Intelligence helps in military operations, and indeed in any endeavour in which men compete, but the rest is risk and choice.

---

[15] Peter Bernstein, Against the Gods. *The Remarkable Story of Risk,* John Wiley, New York, 1996, p.8.

What are military leaders leading for? What is the desired effect of a military operation? Military professionals returning from Iraq and Afghanistan inform me that living in those countries amongst the population and doing what they do - fighting, generating security, reconciling peoples and reconstructing nations - is often a mixture of real, and surreal, experience. They tell me their real measure of success, not found amongst the just war criteria, is 'to bring everyone home'. The mission recedes. Reminiscent of the Grand old Duke of York perhaps, marching up and down the hill? Our armed forces do a serious job: many do not make it home unscathed. In the event too many have died to deliver for other people the hypothesis called liberal democracy – a state of unreality for half the world. Can democracy really be imposed as true fact in lands we don't understand, a hope of dreamlike inconsequence?

So what is it all about? How do our people, the good guys, win? Is there ever a happy ending? As the tipping-point adage has is, does 'victory depend on a single moment and that moment is the triumph of one thought over another'[16]? Tolstoy writes too of 'the moment of moral hesitation that decides the fate of battles'[17]. In that he confirms Clausewitz's recognition that there are moral forces in war, which are psychological and cultural. They are about the strength of opposing wills and such forces have little to do with ethics, [18] which is about universal goodness. In short triumphalism, even 'winning' a war is not the way of the modern liberal democratic spirit. The exit from Afghanistan of NATO forces, we are told by US commanding General John Allen,[19] 'will not be marked by a parade'. Campaigns and wars are missions now. Missions are to be achieved as a matter of belief, not merely won.

I suspect military leaders, and we ourselves as bystanders, have to think intuitively, counter-intuitively and counter-counter-intuitively to make any

---

[16] Quoted by Henry Lachouque in his Introduction to Napoleon Bonaparte, *The Waterloo Campaign*, Folio Society, London, 1957,p.21.

[17] Leo Tolstoy, *War and Peace*, (1869), Oxford University Press, 1991, p.196

[18] See commentary on Clausewitz, by G.F. Henderson, *Science of War*, Longmans Green, London, 1906, pp 173-174.

[19] *The Times*, 11 February 2013. A poignant flag hauling down ceremonial, as invented by the British signalling withdrawal from Empire, is likely.

sense at all of our world. As Carroll noted 'plenty of choice, only make up your mind. Now what do you want?' Again simplify at least some of all that algebra and maybe a leader is on the way to being effective in achieving success in peace and war, at whatever level, strategic, operational or tactical.

After these lengthy introductory sections, including glimpses of wisdom amid chaos in the Lewis Carroll - Charles Dodgson novels, the rest of this paper is about leaders and leading in the context today's armed forces. To make sense of the potentially chaotic looking-glass battlefield I chosen two well-known classic authors, great theorists and intellectual leaders in their own right, John Adair and Howard Gardner. I believe they can help lead the way.

Howard Gardner's research

'Stories about the self, stories about the group, stories about values and meaning'[20].

The expert of multiple intelligences,[21] the developmental psychologist Howard Gardner, wrote a book in 1997 which is not very well known outside the USA. He studies eleven leaders, national and political, religious and military, of science and learning. Of twentieth century international influence they are top leaders in their fields.

Gardner's book should studied by all thinking leaders. What is so striking about his book are the quite simple findings and interpretations of how effective leaders succeed. A man himself of some humility, Gardner does not claim that what he writes can inform every sort of leader, in every sort of context and level of influence. I disagree. In my view he has exposed clearly and exactly the truth about how leaders do what they do and their real effectiveness through engaging the energies and lives of others.

---

[20] Howard Gardner, *Leading Minds. An anatomy of Leadership,* Harper Collins, London 1996, New York 1997, p. 50.

[21] Howard Gardner, *Frames of Mind* , Fontana, London, 1993.

'A leader', Gardner writes, 'is an individual (or, rarely, a set of individuals), who significantly affects the thoughts, feelings, and / or behaviors of a significant number of individuals. Most leaders are "direct"; they address their public face to face. But I have called attention to an unrecognized phenomenon – indirect leadership: in this variety of leading, individuals exert impact through the works they create'[22].

'Whether direct or indirect', Gardner continues,

'leaders fashion stories – principally stories of identity. It is important that a leader be a good story teller, but equally crucial that the leader embody that story in his or her life. When a leader tells stories to experts, the stories can be quite sophisticated; but when the leader is dealing with a diverse, heterogeneous group, the story must be sufficiently elemental to be understood by the untutored, or "unschooled" mind'.

Gardner analyses with great insight and balance leaders like Mahatma Ghandi and Margaret Thatcher; Martin Luther King and Pope John XXII; Alfred P. Sloan, the business leader and George C. Marshall, who identified 'the good soldier'. He investigates Jean Monnet, architect of European unity, and the leaders on all sides in World War 2, juxtaposing Churchill and Hitler, Roosevelt and Stalin. While concentrating on great figures, in his preface Gardner encourages his findings to be used amongst the 'more normal forms of leadership' as a creative activity, by implication involving close teams created with 'an identity' and sustained by the leader. At that point he stops.

Gardner is known currently to be working on a ninth intelligence, 'existential intelligence'. This accords with Carroll's heroine's sense of

---

[22] Howard Gardner, 1996, p. xiii.

'disorientation and confusion in the face of an apparently meaningless and absurd world', to quote one of many definitions of existentialism. It is also about 'identity', which in his leadership book he links with story-telling. However one has to be careful not to confuse substance with method. Gardner's eight (or nine) intelligences are chiefly means of personal self-analysis and introspection in a complex even chaotic world.

Readers will quickly interpret the author's method for a wide array of people in positions of leadership, working with many different sorts of teams. Leaders need

- To live and work among others, inspiring and influencing their thoughts and emotions for specific human enterprises in the real world;
- To find and articulate a deliberate and coherent narrative, a story, a chronology of beginning, middle and end, as succinct an interpretation of the realities to faced and future to be attained;
- To enable themselves and their followers to embody and personify the story, with a sense of self-direction, self-discipline and identity amongst all persons involved;
- To create themselves, or help create, enduring works with a long-term purpose.

Gardner rightly recognizes that human beings love stories, acted according to a pre-determined chronology of cause and effect, of dramatic events, interesting relationships of *dramatis personae* characters, 'each man playing his part', and circumstances that set the mood of excitement, humour or catharsis. Tales with happy endings or a moral are favoured. In living out a story people do not choose a tragic ending, but will live and strive to prevent or curb tragedy. The stories must be authentic and have integrity to be believed. They have to foretell the future. They can be self-fulfilling. The greatest feats of leadership are. Above all, stories should be made to come true.

As works of imagination Gardner's thesis is that leaders create, manage or manipulate these stories[23] to stimulate imagination in others. The specific enterprise 'appropriate environment' or context, Adair suggests (see footnote 1.) a leader needs to consider other numerous factors. Among them are the level of sophistication; the heterogeneity of the group including schooled and unschooled minds; the sheer numbers of people involved; and the dynamics and complexity of the enterprise / story. Capturing peoples' imagination and holding it , is the greatest contribution leaders make, beyond all other mental and physical exertions.

Action-centred leadership - John Adair

'The real aim ought to be to develop character, and that can only be done by leading'.[24] Edward W. Benson (1829 - 1896).

If leading is a universal phenomenon, we can link it to what Kant described as the categorical imperative. Leading is an imperative without which many tasks fail. Thus it is a self-defining activity, which exists because it is creative. It is a reasoning activity and a personal activity, combining the objective and the subjective.

Professor John Adair instituted leadership development thinking and training at the Royal Military Academy Sandhurst in 1963. In his book ten years later he termed his approach to how leaders lead as 'action centred'. Even if the leadership is cerebral, it is still doing something which provokes action and movement in others. As noted already 'good leadership', he writes,[25] always exists in a form appropriate to its environment', its context. Contexts we know are more complicated than they were when Adair started writing and

---

[23] Leaders such as Martin Luther King and Jean Monnet with positive and humane agendas are juxtaposed with the powerfully distorted creativity / destructiveness of Hitler's and Stalin's narratives. The imaginative visions they created were found out sooner or later to be sad and evil delusions.

[24] A.C.Benson quoting his educationalist father Archbishop E.W.Benson, in *Along the Road*, John Murray, London, 1913, p. 376.

[25] John Adair, *Training for Leadership*, Macdonald, London 1968, his first of many books on the subject.

developing leaders. A context is a context, simple or complex. We now have to assume they are almost always more complex than at first they appear, hence my lengthy introductory sections.

As an objective activity John Adair writes of the 'task' and the commodities or assets needed to complete the task. The subjective 'needs' are how the individuals, whether few in number in a tight team, or many in the community, are affected, and what are their individual needs to make them effective team members. His third set of needs are group or 'team needs', the needs of the team to be built and maintained as an entirety, an integrated whole. This latter set of needs is frequently extremely difficult to bring together, as many teams and communities are large in number and very diverse. This is where the leader rises above his or her command and management position to make the enterprise effective and successful. Adair teaches leaders to generate a true sense of 'integration', the making of one, as shown in his well-known diagram[26] from his many books.

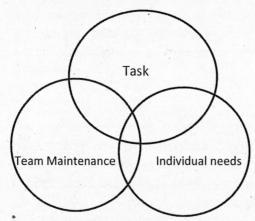

The needs within in circle are of course groups of a large number of variables, in this case demanding to be dependent variables. In later books, Adair specifies the three as 'achieving the task', 'building and maintaining the team' and 'developing the individual'. (He has moved from nouns to verbal

---

[26] John Adair, op. cit. 1968, p.18.

expression, being stronger.) Throughout all his writings, the author believes personal example in the leader is paramount. 'Lead, follow or get out of the way' style is a rarity, to be used only in acute emergency. Consensus is all and this leads to further investigation of the notion of integrity. The best form of leading inspires continuing goodwill. In that sense leading is an ethical exercise.

The search for integrity

'Integrity …. means adherence to a set of moral, artistic or other values, especially truth, that are so to speak outside oneself'.[27] John Adair.

In a previous Sandhurst *Occasional Paper*, I ended by writing 'We are still looking for a true definition of integrity'[28]. Maybe it too is a thesaurus rather than a dictionary word. Anyway the quest for integrity in matching cause and effect is the chief 'task need' for any leader under any circumstances. The opposites and contradictions leaders face somehow have to be united, and simplified as Heraclitus noted, in the 'change' process. That is another feature of leading; managing the process and dynamics of change, usually and additionally implying risk.

In a later book Adair writes of the needs which the leader should develop in the individual. The same word 'integrity' recurs and he investigates Confucius's writings on the subject. 'A person of integrity', Adair judges, 'then is honest to such a degree that they are incapable of being false to a trust, responsibility or pledge –or to their own standards of conduct'[29]. Such is a judgement of character, the development of which in team members and in others more widely is a leader's responsibility.

---

[27] John Adair, *Confucius on Leadership*, Macmillan, Basingstoke, 2013, p. 111
[28] Patrick Mileham, 'Fit and Proper Persons; Officership Revisited', Sandhurst Occasional No 10, 2012, p. 17.
[29] John Adair, op cit. , 2013, p. 111.

Assuming the leader himself or herself is a person of integrity, the search for integrity in other persons and teams is teams is endless. Leaders look for people of character. Effective leaders develop character in others, fulfilling an individual's 'need' and by extension, a 'team need'.

What is personal integrity, the goodness in people, their innate or tutored grasp of what is universally not narrowly ethical? Looking to its Greek roots, *ethos, ethikos* starts with individual character. Strength of character has an inextricable dependent variable, conscience[30]. Integrity, at the personal level, is that faculty of our character whereby what we say, we do; what we promise we deliver; what we believe in - in all conscience - we practise openly in our lives; our private behaviour and our inner thoughts are outwardly manifest in actions of good faith. Moreover what we say we will not do, for good reason, we do not do. Shakespeare had words for it too.

'This above all: to thine own self be true,

And it must follow as the night the day,

Thou canst not be false to any man'.[31]

On the face of it this seems deliberately paradoxical. However, a person of character and integrity must have a sense of altruism and conscience. Genuine and sincere, he must be at one with himself so he can be at one with others. Truth and integrity go together, so does trust; the opposites are duplicity and selfishness. A leader then is a person who generates trust, trusts others and by them in turn is trusted. Give and take, trust is the currency, how a leader and the led value each other.

Are leaders effective? Success is the ultimate test, sooner rather than later. The leader must somehow deliver the story faithfully, not falsely. One mistake may be allowable, but people do not follow a leader after two failed

---

[30] '...men of reason and conscience', Article 1 of the Universal Declaration of Human Rights states that we....
[31] William Shakespeare, *Hamlet,* Act I, scene 3, lines 78-80

tasks or when the story, the predetermined task, falls apart, disintegrates, particularly when lives are at stake. That having been said, there are likely or manifest tensions, strains and divisions inherent in all teams, whatever the task. Team integrity, cohesion is literally vital.

Taking account of both Gardner's creative and imaginative story and Adair's advice to grasp the task, firmly linking causes with effects, military professionals should 'create' (the opposite of destroy) three things

- Preparations for the use of armed force;
- Violence if necessary, to eliminate violence during operations;
- Lasting peace.

Looking to the creative task, does the Heraclitan unity of opposites include the enemy? The answer is yes and Shakespeare again has the answer.

'A peace is of the nature of a conquest,

For then both parties nobly are subdued,

And neither party loser'.[32]

This act is creative and imaginative. If achieved it is an act, maybe the supreme act, of leadership, when a former enemy trusts you enough, as Clausewitz suggests, to do your will.[33]

How do military leaders lead enemies / potential friends, in order to collaborate in the same story which leads to peace? What's the purpose of war, of leadership and of teamwork amongst military professionals if it doesn't have the peace of the world as an ending, sometime, to the unfolding 'story' of mankind? Integrity, oneness with a former enemy, is what creates lasting peace.

---

[32] William Shakespeare, *Henry IV part 2*, Act IV, scene 2, lines 89-91.
[33] Karl von Clausewitz, *On War*, ed. Michael Howard and Peter Paret, Princeton, NJ, 1976, p.75

Synthesis

This short paper can address many but answer only a few questions. There is no space for examples and case-studies. Many are to be found in a number of leadership guides published since 2009 by the Armed Forces[34]. They are chiefly 'descriptive'. The intuition in Britain, rightly or wrongly, is that strong 'normative' and prescriptive rules for leaders do not work. Leadership is algebra not arithmetic. Too often dependent variables seem to change into independent variables, or vice versa, in looking-glass style.

I re-emphasize that leaders must clarify causes and effects in their own minds before they can lead others effectively. Recent military operations have been conducted by thousands of leaders within hundreds of thousands of local stories. Such have been part of the national stories of the Balkans, Iraq and Afghanistan. Any difficulties have been compounded by the lack of task definition (in Adair's meaning), and the absence of a properly articulated sense of story (as Gardner indicates is necessary). But is task definition and management of historical progress beyond any individual leader rising from within the constraints of liberal democracies? History is made at grass-root level where life is lived, not in the imagination of future historians.

Bringing together Howard Gardner's and John Adair's analysis and advice, leaders can be developed to understand how better to lead, and followers consent more readily to play their part with determination. There are three points synthesizing the two authors' insight.

- The task, the activity, the enterprise needs to unfold as a story, with beginning, middle and a culminating end point. We would like to think this story is the campaign strategy. We can refer to the integrity, the wholeness of a task. This is to be formed powerfully by the leaders national and military. The series of operational deployments in Iraq (OP TELIC 1-13) and in Afghanistan (OP HERRICK, currently no. 19 in June 2013) are themselves unfolding 'stories', like acts in a play. How consequential such acts have been with a strong, coherent strategic imagination at work leading to a

---

[34] Andrew St George's *Way of Leadership. The Royal Navy*, Preface, Random House, London 2012; *Developing Leaders. A Sandhurst Guide,* Royal Military Academy Sandhurst, Camberley, 2012; *Leadership, An Anthology,* 2nd edn., Royal Air Force Leadership Centre, Cranwell, 2009.

satisfactory end, can be questioned. War is more than imitative drama, it is a real life and death struggle. To succeed armed force has to be creative in the end, and this is a matter for politicians and statesmen. Leaders at all levels have to make it all work and bring success. In all senses of the word, the task, the story must be made to 'come true'.

- Individual needs are those of 'identity', with people's and team members 'thoughts and emotions' engaged consensually. They have to embody the story as much as the leader does. The full panoply of human resource management, employment law and provisions expressed in such a device as a 'military covenant', form the basis of morale and confidence, but only so far. Leaders have to inspire and capture the imagination of individuals, inducing willing and sustained collaboration.

- 'Team maintenance', the integrating of individuals fighting for each other in the 'story' that is the unit history over time beyond the individuals themselves, forms the basis of 'moral cohesion'[35] which effective leaders should generate and sustain. This is what the regimental system in the Army as experienced amongst the smallest groupings leading to the integrity of the whole, is all about. Similarly moral cohesion is what leads to the 'good ship' syndrome in the Royal Navy, and the strength of character above professional expertise in squadrons of the Royal Air Force

In conclusion one can never be definite about what leaders do. The context in which they operate so often involves the dynamics of human nature of other people interacting with their own character. Groups might act together with integrity, but in the end they comprise unique individuals. There are skills, means and methods open to leaders to use. There is common sense and a vast array of research on leadership available. There is advice on ethical conduct, pragmatism and practical wisdom, as well as the classic virtues of courage, wise judgement, justice and restraint. The point of being a leader is that he or she is unique. That is where leadership begins and sensible advice ends.

---

[35] Ministry of Defence, *British Defence Doctrine*, 2011, section 4-7.